The Grand Mosque of Paris

A Story of How Muslims Rescued Jews During the Holocaust

by KAREN GRAY RUELLE AND
DEBORAH DURLAND DESAIX

Holiday House / *New York*

"Save one life, and it is as if you've saved all of humanity."

—Islamic hadith and Jewish proverb

Text and illustrations copyright © 2009 by Karen Gray Ruelle and Deborah Durland DeSaix
All Rights Reserved
HOLIDAY HOUSE is registered in the U.S. Patent and Trademark Office.
Printed and Bound in July 2015 at Tien Wah Press, Johor Bahru, Johor, Malaysia
The text typeface is Garamond 3.
The artwork was created with oil paint applied with brushes, paper towels, and all twenty fingers.
www.holidayhouse.com

5 7 9 10 8 6

Library of Congress Cataloging-in-Publication Data
Ruelle, Karen Gray.
The grand mosque of Paris : a story of how Muslims rescued Jews during the Holocaust /
by Karen Gray Ruelle and Deborah Durland DeSaix. — 1st ed.
p. cm.
ISBN 978-0-8234-2159-6 (hardcover)
1. World War, 1939-1945—Jews—Rescue—France—Paris. 2. Holocaust, Jewish (1939-1945) —France—Paris.
3. Righteous Gentiles in the Holocaust—France—Paris. 4. Jewish-Arab relations. 5. France—Ethnic relations.
I. DeSaix, Deborah Durland. II. Title.
D804.65.R84 2008
940.53'18350944361—dc22
2008017209
ISBN 978-0-8234-2304-0 (paperback)

In 1940 war came to Paris, and life was turned upside down. Nazis in heavy boots tramped the streets, people waited in long lines for hours just to buy a small loaf of bread, and policemen arrested whole families for the crime of being Jewish.

During the war, fear, hunger, and loss became everyday companions. Danger was everywhere, especially for Jews, including Jewish children. Germany's Nazis, who had started the war, hated Jews and were determined to hunt them down.

Nazi soldiers invaded Poland in 1939, and World War II began, spreading the Nazi regime across Europe. Many Jews fled to France, where they hoped they would be safe. Then, in 1940, the Nazis conquered France. A new French government of collaborators was set up in the city of Vichy. The Vichy government, working hand in hand with the Nazis, immediately began to pass anti-Jewish laws.

The Vichy police arrested Jews and crowded them into filthy, vermin-infested internment camps. But a plan of truly unimaginable horror was looming. In 1942, the Nazis set up death camps, and began the mass murder of Europe's Jews. The Vichy government rounded up Jews of all ages and sent them to the death camps. In France 11,402 Jewish children, toddlers, and even tiny babies were deported to death camps. Only about three hundred of them survived the war.

Throughout France, some people tried to protect Jewish children, hiding them in convents and schools, on farms and at hospitals, anywhere a Jewish child might be able to blend in. But in Paris, Nazis and police were everywhere, and it was much harder to hide.

For the first two years of the Occupation, the southern part of France was controlled by Vichy rather than the Nazis. In spite of the Vichy police, the Southern Zone was still a safer place for Jews than the Nazi-occupied Northern Zone. Many Jewish families attempted to make the perilous trip south.

Some Jews in Paris found help in an extraordinary place. It was the Grand Mosque, the center of the Islamic community in France, an oasis hidden behind high walls right in the middle of the city.

The Grand Mosque shimmered like a mirage, the white domes and the glittering mosaics of the minaret in stark contrast to the muted colors of Paris. When the mosque was built in 1926, the North African countries of Algeria, Morocco, and Tunisia were under French rule, and many Muslims had come to Paris from those countries. The land for the mosque was given by the French government, in exchange for a symbolic payment of one franc, to thank the half-million Muslim soldiers who had fought for France during the First World War.

Expert craftsmen who were brought over from North Africa created the mosque's intricate carvings and richly patterned mosaics. Graceful columns and arches surrounded courtyards and gardens filled with flowers, trees, and cascading fountains. The song of birds was everywhere.

From the top of the minaret, the voice of the muezzin could be heard across the neighborhood, calling the faithful to prayer five times each day. But the mosque was not only a place to pray. It was created as a true community center. Everything that happened in its Muslim community was recorded at the mosque, including births, marriages, and deaths. Adults and children studied there, and could consult the many precious manuscripts and books in the library. On alternating days, men or women could relax in the steam bath of the hammam. Children could play in the gardens, adults could stroll along the tiled walkways or shop in the souk, and all were welcome for mint tea and sweet North African pastries in the mosque's restaurant.

Any Muslim in need could find help at the mosque. There was even a clinic within the mosque's grounds, and a hospital in the suburbs for those who were seriously ill, with an Islamic cemetery nearby.

The man at the heart of the mosque was its rector, Si Kaddour Benghabrit. As rector, he was in charge of running the mosque, while the imam was the spiritual leader. A sophisticated and cultured Algerian-born diplomat, Si Benghabrit wrote plays and books, and loved music. He had been an important official in Morocco, and had worked closely with many French diplomats. Si Benghabrit was equally comfortable in Paris and North Africa, and he was the perfect choice to be the mosque's first rector. Si Benghabrit was the most powerful Muslim in France, and the French government looked to him to speak for the entire Muslim community.

Then France fell to the Nazis. In September 1940, just three months later, the Nazis and the Vichy government already suspected that the people of the mosque were helping Jews. This put the mosque's rector and his staff in great peril, but it didn't stop them.

Salim Halali, a young Berber Jew from Algeria, was trapped in Paris during the Occupation. He had come to the city when he was fourteen to fulfill his dream of becoming a singer. Now, in grave danger, he came to the mosque. Si Benghabrit made a Certificate of Conversion to show the Nazis, "proving" that Salim's grandfather had converted to Islam. The rector even had a stonecarver secretly inscribe the family name on an unmarked tombstone in the Muslim cemetery, hoping to convince the Nazis that Salim was actually a Muslim.

Jewish or Muslim, the people of North Africa lived as neighbors and shared similar cultures. Through the centuries, they referred to each other as brothers. They also looked very much alike. That's why Salim was able to live safely in the mosque for the rest of the war, pretending to be a Muslim.

Two friends from North Africa escaped from a prisoner-of-war camp in Germany and made their way to Paris. Albert Assouline, a Jew, and Yassa Rahal, a Muslim, had no identity papers and were certain to be arrested if caught. Because Albert was Jewish, the risk for him was even greater.

The two men had to stay hidden and tried to find refuge at a place of worship. "We ruled out the synagogue," said Albert. "The church didn't seem safe either, so we ended up at the door of the [Grand] Mosque of Paris. He went in first, leaving me outside, and asked if he could bring in a friend who was not a Muslim. They said yes, so he came back out for me and we stayed for two or three days." While he was there, Albert saw other people in hiding. He said, "The adults were in the basement, and the children were in apartments upstairs. Si Kaddour Benghabrit had a large family and they were sheltering children. In the other apartments there were children, too, who could have been Jewish or not."

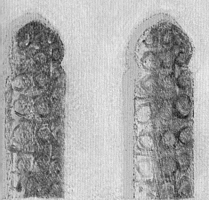

Besides all the public rooms of the mosque, there were the apartments for the people who worked there: the rector, the imam, the muezzin, the custodian, and others. Many of them had families and could hide North African Jewish children in among their own. Nobody would notice the difference, and even if they did, the mosque could provide false Muslim birth certificates. It would be nearly impossible for anyone to check their authenticity because records in North Africa were too disorganized.

However, only people who were Muslims or who could pass as North African Muslims could stay at the mosque for more than a few days. Most others had to be guided out of Paris fairly quickly. It would be too difficult to keep them hidden from the Nazis.

Nazis and Vichy officials treated the mosque with respect, but they could come in and investigate at the slightest suspicion that anyone might be hiding there. Fortunately, there was an alarm system. Sitting in his office, Si Benghabrit could discreetly press a button on the floor under his desk that set off the alarm in another part of the mosque.

Once warned, the people in hiding rushed into the secluded women's section of the prayer room, where even Nazis and Vichy police dared not enter. The rector delayed the search by demanding that the soldiers and police remove their boots. Before going into the prayer room of any mosque, it is customary to remove all footwear. Taking off heavy military boots took time, giving everyone the opportunity to get out of sight.

The Nazis were reluctant to target Muslims. They feared a Muslim uprising in North Africa, where they were already fighting the Allies. Even so, as Albert wrote, "There were some close calls, like the day when the Germans were astonished to smell tobacco at the mosque, even though they knew Muslims were forbidden {by their religion} to smoke."

18

Dr. Ahmed Somia, a Muslim from Tunisia, tried to protect children at risk of Nazi arrest. He pretended that they were ill and sent them to special clinics away from Paris, where they would be safe until the war ended. Sometimes he was able to give them false identity papers. This would disguise a Jewish child as a Christian or a Muslim.

At the Muslim hospital where Dr. Somia worked, doctors secretly treated injured Allied pilots and parachutists at night, and hid them during the day. Some of these men had come to France as spies. Others had been shot down by Nazis while flying missions over France. They were behind enemy lines, and they needed help.

"During the war," Dr. Somia said, "we formed a group to aid North African prisoners of war who had escaped. . . . We were there to help anyone who was persecuted or hunted, who needed a place to hide, . . . and we could direct them to the mosque, especially, which was always open to them. There were many who followed that route, and found shelter at the mosque."

One person who needed shelter was a Tunisian Jew. He came to Paris on business, and then disappeared. Nobody knew what had happened to him, and his family feared he was dead. Two and a half years later, after the end of the war, he returned home at last. He said that he had been hiding from the Nazis and had found shelter at the mosque. He was living there all that time, and told his boss that he spent his days improving his Arabic.

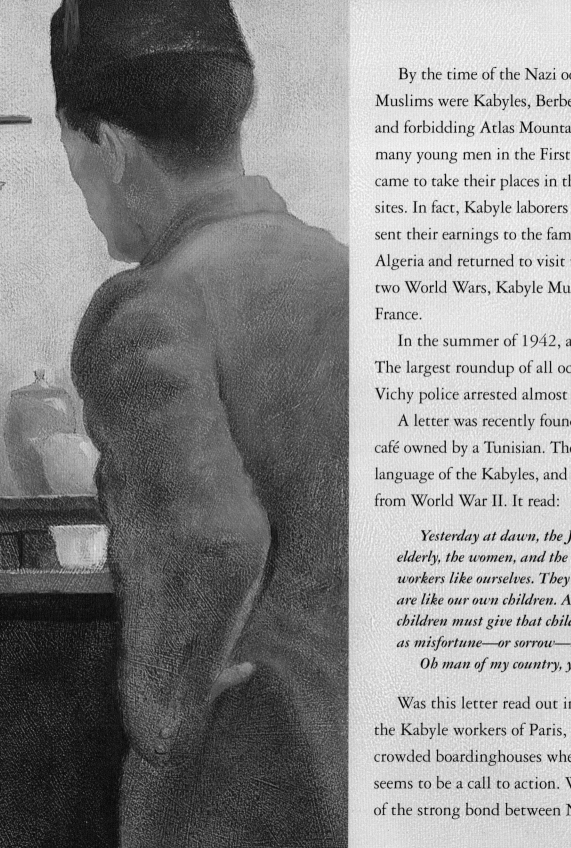

By the time of the Nazi occupation, nearly all of Paris's Muslims were Kabyles, Berbers from Kabylia, up in the high and forbidding Atlas Mountains of Algeria. After France lost many young men in the First World War, workers from Kabylia came to take their places in the factories and on construction sites. In fact, Kabyle laborers built the Paris subways. These men sent their earnings to the families they'd had to leave behind in Algeria and returned to visit them when they could. Between the two World Wars, Kabyle Muslims became part of the fabric of France.

In the summer of 1942, arrests of Jews in France escalated. The largest roundup of all occurred in Paris in July, when the Vichy police arrested almost thirteen thousand Jews at once.

A letter was recently found among the old papers of a Paris café owned by a Tunisian. The letter was written in Kabyle, the language of the Kabyles, and the café owner said that it dated from World War II. It read:

> *Yesterday at dawn, the Jews of Paris were arrested. The elderly, the women, and the children. In exile like ourselves, workers like ourselves. They are our brothers. Their children are like our own children. Anyone who encounters one of his children must give that child shelter and protection for as long as misfortune—or sorrow—lasts.*
>
> *Oh man of my country, your heart is generous.*

Was this letter read out in the café? Did it circulate among the Kabyle workers of Paris, making its way through the crowded boardinghouses where these men lived? It certainly seems to be a call to action. Without a doubt, it is a recognition of the strong bond between North African Muslims and Jews.

Many Muslims in the French Resistance were involved in helping Jews escape from Nazi-occupied Paris. The Resistance was a clandestine network of spies and fighters, made up of ordinary people—perhaps teachers, bakers, journalists, or factory workers—who did whatever they could to fight the Nazis.

The Kabyles who fought in the French Resistance had two advantages. The first was their language. Nobody but Kabyles spoke or understood it. They were able to form a tight network and use Kabyle as a kind of code. Dr. Somia said, ". . . You could confide a secret to a Kabyle and rest absolutely assured that it would not be betrayed."

The second advantage was the fact that the Kabyles were Muslim. When they wore the traditional tasseled wool felt hat—called a checheya or a fez—it signaled that they were Muslim, and so they were less likely to be stopped by the Nazis. This also made the checheya a perfect disguise for some Jews.

Kabyles operated a secret network that smuggled people out of Paris to safety, and they also carried coded messages between the Resistance in France and the Free French Army in Algeria. Their smuggling network was initially devised to aid escaped prisoners of war, and Allied pilots and parachutists in hiding. However, as the war went on, the Kabyles began to smuggle more and more Jewish men, women, and children away from danger. One route they used to help people escape the Nazis involved the mosque. They would sneak people into the mosque right before curfew, when the police were distracted by their dinner. A story describes a deliveryman and his vehicle, a three-wheeled bicycle with a large bin attached to it. There was just enough space inside the bin to hide someone. As long as nobody looked inside, that hidden person might be safe. The deliveryman could pedal to the mosque through the streets of Paris, right under the noses of the police.

There were other ways to slip people into the mosque. Albert said, "You could enter through secret doors into the basement, the hammam, or through the mosque's restaurant."

Once they had been smuggled into the mosque, people usually didn't stay for long.

In the subbasement of the mosque there was a cramped stairway leading down into a maze of tunnels. Centuries before, as Paris was built, stone was quarried beneath the city to construct its magnificent buildings. This left behind a *souterrain*—a subterranean tangle of interconnecting tunnels, rooms, and passageways, eventually including an underground river, and burial chambers called the Catacombs.

The ceilings of the souterrain's passageways were low. In some places a person would have to crouch down or even crawl to get through. Rough steps led down to deeper levels, and there were holes that could swallow an unwary traveler.

Hundreds of miles of utterly dark, chilly passageways twisted and turned beneath the streets. If you knew the route, you could travel underground from the mosque to the bank of the river Seine. If you didn't know the way, you could become hopelessly lost in the souterrain

The Kabyle Resistance guided people through the black labyrinth of the souterrain, from the mosque to the bank of the Seine near the Halles aux Vins—a huge central wine market. Wine was delivered here in massive wooden barrels from all over France. The barrels were transported on long *péniches*—barges—and returned empty.

These péniches were used by the Kabyle Resistance to carry their coded messages. Among the empty wine barrels on board they hid people—Allied pilots and parachutists, escaped prisoners of war, Resistance fighters, and Jews. Gliding out into the current, the péniches would transport their precious cargo, spiriting to safety those who had been sheltered in the Grand Mosque of Paris.

Throughout the war, Si Kaddour Benghabrit had to maintain a precarious and dangerous balance. As rector of the mosque, he was obliged to deal with the Nazis and the Vichy government in order to protect the Muslim community in Paris. But during the Occupation he also continued to secretly allow the mosque to be a safe haven for those who needed it.

The Allies chased the Nazis out of Paris in September 1944 after four long years of occupation. World War II ended the following year. Si Benghabrit continued as rector of the mosque until his death in 1954. His grave lies in the mosque, where he was buried facing in the direction of Mecca, as are all Muslims.

Because of Si Benghabrit's actions, the Jewish singer Salim Halali lived a long, successful life and is still revered as the father of modern North African song.

Albert Assouline, the Jewish Algerian who had escaped from a prisoner-of-war camp, joined the Free French Army in Algeria and battled the Nazis until the end of the war. Afterward he settled in Paris. For the rest of his life, he was dedicated to helping people in need at the Grand Mosque, where his own life had been saved.

After the war the Muslim Tunisian doctor Ahmed Somia continued just as he had always done, saving lives regardless of his patient's politics or beliefs. He almost never spoke of his actions during the Occupation.

Muslims working in the mosque and in the Resistance saved numerous lives—Jewish and non-Jewish—by their selfless acts. They risked their own lives to do what they felt was right. It should never be forgotten that Muslims came to the aid of their brothers and sisters, the Jews. Amid the horror of the Holocaust, something noble and courageous quietly unfolded within the walls of the Grand Mosque of Paris.

AFTERWORD

This is a little-known story that is shrouded in mystery. Writing about clandestine events that took place at a time of turmoil involving people who had an oral rather than a written tradition, and with many of the participants having now passed away, presents many difficulties. There is very little written about the brave acts of the Muslims of Paris during World War II, and almost nothing in the official archives. Because these activities were clandestine, they would not have been documented by the authorities anyway—unless they had failed. However, there are some stories that have been preserved, and we've tracked down as many of them as we could.

We began by trying, unsuccessfully, to locate Jews who had been saved at the mosque. Later we learned that others had conducted similar searches in recent years. As far as we know, no new firsthand testimonies have been found, although some secondhand references have turned up. Sixty-three years after the end of the war (at the time of this writing), it's not surprising. Salim Halali, Albert Assouline, and Dr. Ahmed Somia have all passed away. Even those who were children at the time of the war would now be elderly. Also, it seems clear that most people who were sheltered at the mosque only stayed for a brief time, as little as several days, or perhaps even several hours. The mosque was generally a place of temporary rather than long-term refuge, with some notable exceptions. In addition, Martine Bernheim, vice president of LICRA (Ligue Internationale Contre le Racisme et l'Antisemitisme), speculates that children staying in or passing through the mosque might never have realized where they were. Adults would not have told them, for fear of exposure by a child who might not understand the need for secrecy. Even adults who spent a short time hiding in the mosque might not remember, decades later, that small part of what was surely the most traumatic time of their lives.

Derri Berkani, a French filmmaker and novelist of Algerian descent whose parents were both in the Kabyle Resistance, began researching this story in 1974. He interviewed a number of people, including Dr. Somia, Mr. Assouline, and former members of the Kabyle Resistance. He also spoke with Mrs. Lamberger, now deceased, a Jewish woman who recounted to him her escape from occupied Paris as a girl hidden on a péniche operated by a Kabyle. In the archive of the Grand Mosque, Mr. Berkani and his film crew discovered additional evidence in a register of children's names. By his count, for the Muslim population between 1940 and 1944, there was an excess of about four hundred children on the list. He believes these were Jewish children given protective Muslim identities. When he returned some years later, however, the register was nowhere to be found.

Mr. Berkani described this to us in our interviews with him. His 1990 documentary, *Une Résistance Oubliée: La Mosquée*, presents a large part of the story he uncovered.

Estimates of the number of people saved at the mosque vary widely. In his book *Among the Righteous: Lost Stories from the Holocaust's Long Reach into Arab Lands*, Robert Satloff describes his meeting with the current rector of the Grand Mosque. Rector Dalil Boubakeur told him that up to one hundred North African Jews were given certificates of Muslim identity at the mosque, thereby saving their lives. But Albert Assouline wrote in his article in *Almanach du Combattant*, "Not less than 1,732 resistants found refuge in its [the mosque's] basements: escaped Muslim prisoners of war, but also Christians and Jews. These last were by far the most numerous." Mr. Berkani told us that Mr. Assouline determined that number when he returned to the mosque after the war. He counted 1,732 extra stubs from ration cards among the mosque's records for the time of the Occupation. This led him to assert that at least that number of people had been sheltered at the mosque.

Our research took us to various archives and libraries in Paris and one in Aix-en-Provence, but we turned up very little of use. We were denied entry to the mosque's archive. Fortunately, one document of note was discovered by Mrs. Bernheim and a colleague in the archive of the Ministry of Foreign Affairs. It was an official Vichy memo dated September 24, 1940, and addressed directly to the minister. It informed him that the Nazis suspected the personnel of the Grand Mosque of providing false certificates of Muslim identity to Jews in order to protect them. It also stated that the imam of the mosque had been summoned and ordered to stop this practice immediately. Written just three months after the Occupation began, this document is powerful evidence.

It's most likely too late now to speak with anyone who was there when these events took place. It seems that many of the details of this story are destined to remain forever uncertain, with few facts proven to a historian's satisfaction. All we have are tantalizing pieces that we believe, when put together, provide convincing evidence: The lives of Jews were saved by the Muslims of the Grand Mosque of Paris.

GLOSSARY

Allah—The Islamic name for God

Allies—Armed forces from the United States, France, Great Britain, and the Soviet Union, all of whom fought against the Nazis

Berber—The indigenous peoples of North Africa, Berbers predated the Arab Muslims there. While many Berbers have adopted Islam and the Arabic language, many have also retained their original languages and cultures.

checheya or **fez**—A brimless, flat-topped, wool felt hat in red or black with a black tassel on top, often worn by working men from North Africa

franc—The unit of French currency prior to the Euro

Free French Army—French soldiers who continued to fight against the Germans after France fell to Germany. The Free French Army was not part of Vichy France.

hadith—Sayings of the Prophet Muhammad in the Islamic faith

hammam—Bath house containing a Turkish bath or steam bath

The Holocaust—The mass slaughter of six million Jews and many others by the Nazis and their followers during World War II

Kabyle—One of the Berber groups from the Atlas Mountains of Algeria

Mecca—The city where the Prophet Muhammad was born, Mecca is the most holy site in the Muslim world. Muslims are commanded to make a pilgrimage to Mecca at least once in their lives.

minaret—A mosque's tower. The muezzin traditionally calls the faithful to prayer from a balcony at the top of the minaret.

mosque—Muslim place of worship

muezzin—The person whose job it is to call the faithful to prayer through a series of incantations

Prophet Muhammad—The founder of Islam and the Prophet chosen by Allah to reveal his message

souk—Bazaar or marketplace

synagogue—Jewish place of worship

ACKNOWLEDGMENTS

Without Derri Berkani, this story might have been lost forever. We are profoundly grateful to him for generously sharing his insights and knowledge with us. His wonderful film deserves to be shown worldwide. We also thank Annette Herskovits, whose efforts to introduce Mr. Berkani's film to English-speaking viewers and to promote a message of peace and understanding led us to the story of the mosque. She kindly put us in touch with Mr. Berkani and also suggested that we contact Martine Bernheim. Mrs. Bernheim's broad knowledge has been instrumental to our understanding, and we can't possibly thank her enough for all her help.

We owe a debt of thanks to Abdelfettah Halim, a librarian at the Arab World Institute in Paris. His help to us went far beyond the call of duty. Our friend Karen Martinello once again proved invaluable, and we thank her for helping with transcriptions and on-the-ground research, with her trademark generosity and good humor. We also thank the numerous people who helped us in our research and who made time in their busy days to speak with us.

Mary Cash, our editor, has been an enthusiastic supporter of our book, and we thank her for giving us the opportunity to tell this important story.

We want to thank our families for their unflagging support. We very much appreciate their belief in us and in this project.

REFERENCES

All spoken quotes in our text are our translations from the French from Derri Berkani's film, *Une Résistance Oubliée: La Mosquée*. The written quotes are our translations from the French from Albert Assouline's article in *Almanach du Combattant*. Derri Berkani translated the Kabyle letter into French. We based our English version on Annette Herskovits's translation from the French, with her kind permission.

BIBLIOGRAPHY

PUBLICATIONS

Abdi, Nidam. "La chanson maghrébine orphiline." *Liberation* (France) (July 13, 2005).

Archer, Caroline, and Alexandre Parré. *Paris Underground.* New York: Mark Batty, 2005.

Arkoun, Mohammed, ed. *Histoire de l'islam et des musulmans en France du Moyen Âge à nos jours.* Paris: Albin Michel, 2006.

Assouline, Albert. "Une Vocation Ignorée de la Mosquée de Paris." *Almanach du Combattant* (1983): 123–24.

Barnes, Trevor. *Islam: Worship, festivals, and ceremonies from around the world.* World Faiths, Rev. ed. Boston: Kingfisher/Houghton Mifflin, 2005.

Belaïd, Lakhdar. "La Mosquée de Paris: Une Résistance Oubliée." *Islam et Dialogue des Religieux* (France) (June 1995).

Blanchard, Pascal, et al. *Le Paris Arabe.* Paris: Editions La Découverte, 2003.

Bouzeghrane, Nadjia. "Seconde guerre mondiale: Les FTP algériens et le sauvetage d'enfants juifs."*El Watan: Le Quotidien Independant* (France) (May 16, 2005). www.elwatan.com/spip.php?page%20article&id_article%2019338/.

Bouzeghrane, Nadjia. "Si Kaddour Benghabrit, un juste qui mérite reconnaissance." *El Watan: Le Quotidien Independant* (France) (May 16, 2005). www.elwatan.com/spip.php?page%20article&id_article%2019341/.

Boyer, Alain. *L'Institut Musulman de la Mosquée de Paris.* Paris: Centre des Hautes Études sur l'Afrique et l'Asie Modernes, 1992.

Clement, Alain et al. *Atlas du Paris Souterrain.* Paris: Parigramme, 2001.

Courtney-Clarke, Margaret. *Imazighen: The Vanishing Traditions of Berber Women.* With essays by Geraldine Brooks. New York: Clarkson Potter, 1996.

Grieve, Paul. *A Brief Guide to Islam: History, Faith and Politics: The Complete Introduction.* New York: Carroll and Graf, 2006.

Hegedüs, Umar. *Muslim Mosque.* Keystones. London: A & C Black, 2000.

Herskovits, Annette, "The Mosque that Sheltered Jews." *Turning Wheel* (Winter 2004): 21–25.

Klarsfeld, Serge. *French Children of the Holocaust: A Memorial.* New York: New York University Press, 1996.

La Construction Moderne 6 (November 4, 1924): numerous articles.

Macaulay, David. *Mosque.* New York: Houghton Mifflin, 2003.

Marrus, Michael R., and Robert O. Paxton. *Vichy France and the Jews.* Stanford, CA: Stanford University Press, 1995.

McAuliffe, Mary. *Paris Discovered: Explorations in the City of Light.* Hightstown, NJ: Elysian Editions/Princeton Book Company, 2006.

Memmi, Albert. *Portrait du Colonisé, Portrait du Colonisateur.* France: Gallimard, 1985.

Rogasky, Barbara. *Smoke and Ashes: The Story of the Holocaust,* Rev. ed. New York: Holiday House, 2002.

Satloff, Robert. *Among the Righteous: Lost Stories from The Holocaust's Long Reach into Arab Lands.* New York: Public Affairs, 2006.

"Soirée-rencontre du 6 mars." *Bulletin de l'Association Enfants Cachés* (France) (March 2006): 28–32.

Stora, Benjamin, et al. "Dossier: Juifs du Maghreb Entre Orient et Occident." *Archives Juives: Revue d'histoire des Juifs de France* 38, no. 2 (France) (2005).

Wysner, Glora M. *The Kabyle People.* USA: Privately printed, 1945.

FILMS

Berkani, Derri. *Une Résistance Oubliée: La Mosquée.* 1990. ARA/Anabase/AFHIS. 26 min. DVD.

Kupferstein, Daniel. *Les Oubliés de l'Histoire.* DVD.

INTERVIEWS CONDUCTED BY THE AUTHORS IN PARIS, FRANCE

Anonymous. April 11, 2007, and September 26, 2007. (NOTE: This person, who is intimately acquainted with the Grand Mosque, agreed to speak with us only under the condition of anonymity.)

Berkani, Derri (documentary filmmaker and author). Tape recording. April 11, 2007, and September 25, 2007.

Bernheim, Martine (vice president, Ligue Internationale Contre le Racisme et l'Antisémitisme). Tape recording. April 10, 2007, and September 27, 2007.

Derczansky, Annie Paule (founder and president, Les Bâtisseuses de Paix). Tape recording. September 23, 2007.

Gensburger, Sarah (freelance researcher for Yad Vashem). Tape recording. October 2, 2007.

Kanovitch, Dr. Bernard. Tape recording. September 24, 2007.

Salhi, Zouber (official at the Grand Mosque of Paris). October 1, 2007.

Somia, Alain (son of Dr. Ahmed Somia). Tape recording. October 2, 2007.

WEBSITE

www.mosquee-de-paris.org

❋ RECOMMENDED ❋ BOOKS AND FILMS

An asterisk (*) indicates works suitable for young readers.

BOOKS

*Barnes, Trevor. *Islam: Worship, festivals, and ceremonies from around the world.* World Faiths, Rev. ed. Boston: Kingfisher/Houghton Mifflin, 2005.

An accessible, illustrated overview of Islam, this book includes features on Islamic festivals, ceremonies, and art.

*Courtney-Clarke, Margaret. *Imazighen: The Vanishing Traditions of Berber Women.* With essays by Geraldine Brooks. New York: Clarkson Potter, 1996.

The sumptuous photos in this oversized book depict the Berbers— including Kabyles—in their North African homeland, with detailed looks at architecture, weaving, pottery, and the tasks of daily life. In-depth essays accompany this exploration of the Berber culture. For preteens, teens, and adults.

Grieve, Paul. *A Brief Guide to Islam: History, Faith and Politics: The Complete Introduction.* New York: Carroll and Graf, 2006.

This excellent book gives a thorough and clear description of Islam from its beginnings through the present day.

*Macaulay, David. *Mosque.* New York: Houghton Mifflin, 2003.

This beautifully illustrated book for children tells everything there is to know about mosques.

*Rogasky, Barbara. *Smoke and Ashes: The Story of the Holocaust,* Rev. ed. New York: Holiday House, 2002.

This comprehensive book on The Holocaust is appropriate for preteens and teenagers.

Satloff, Robert. *Among the Righteous: Lost Stories from The Holocaust's Long Reach into Arab Lands.* New York: Public Affairs, 2006.

Dr. Satloff is the director of the Washington Institute for Near East Policy. His thoughtful book includes an entire chapter on the Grand Mosque of Paris.

FILMS

*Berkani, Derri. *Une Résistance Oubliée: La Mosquée.* 1990. ARA/Anabase/AFHIS. 26 min. DVD. In French.

Originally made for French television, this documentary is now part of the educational outreach program of the French organization LICRA, the International League Against Racism and Anti-Semitism, and is shown to students in schools across Europe. It tells the story of the Grand Mosque of Paris during World War II. For teens and adults.

*Oury, Gérard. *La Grande Vadrouille.* 1966. Les Films Corona. Videocassette. In French with English subtitles.

This French comedy about British parachutists hiding in France during World War II includes scenes that take place in the hammam of the Grand Mosque of Paris and an escape through the souterrain. For teens and adults.

 INDEX